SCHOOL REFUSAL

Children who are anxious and reluctant to attend school

by
Dr. David Philbrick and Kath Tansey

A NASEN PUBLICATION

Published in 2000

ISBN 1 901485 16 1

Published by NASEN.
NASEN is a registered charity. Charity No. 1007023.
NASEN is a company limited by guarantee, registered in England and Wales. Company No. 2674379.

Further copies of this book and details of NASEN's many other publications may be obtained from the NASEN Bookshop at its registered office: NASEN House, 4/5 Amber Business Village, Amber Close, Amington, Tamworth, Staffs., B77 4RP.
Tel: 01827 311500; Fax: 01827 313005
Email: welcome@nasen.org.uk; Website: www.nasen.org.uk

Copy editing by Nicola von Schreiber.
Cover design by Raphael Creative Design.
Typeset in Times by J. C. Typesetting and printed in the United Kingdom by Newcastle Instant Print.

This booklet was collated and edited by Dr. David Philbrick and Kath Tansey. It is based upon a report produced by a multi-agency working party in Central Durham which was comprised of: a Senior Education Welfare Officer, a Consultant Community Paediatrician, a School Nurse, a Consultant Child and Family Psychiatrist, a Deputy Head Teacher, a Senior Educational Psychologist, and a Team Leader of the Home and Hospital Support Service.

Addresses for Correspondence

Mrs. Kath Tansey
Team Leader
Learning Support Service
Home and Hospital Support Service
Broom Cottages Primary School
Ferryhill
Co. Durham
DL17 8AN
Tel: 01740 652443
Fax: 01740 657792

Dr. David Philbrick
Consultant Child and Family Psychiatrist
The Child and Family Centre
Health Centre
Newcastle Road
Chester-le-Street
Co. Durham
DH3 3UR
Tel: 0191 333 3866
Fax: 0191 333 3868

School Refusal - Children who are anxious and reluctant to attend school

Contents

5

Introduction

Some children with emotional problems may come to the attention of teachers and parents because of difficult or challenging behaviour. Children with emotional problems, without challenging behaviour, may be 'overlooked' and their difficulties may go undetected because they pose no overt management problem. However, if they become anxious or withdrawn and are absent from school for prolonged periods of time, they may be isolated from structures within school, peer group or family that are necessary for their social, emotional and cognitive development.

Existing provision for the needs of children whose anxieties and reluctance to attend school have led to school refusal may be fragmented and uncoordinated. It is intended that this booklet should:

- promote awareness and understanding of the nature of anxious school refusal
- promote recognition of anxious school refusal and appropriate early intervention
- emphasise the central role of schools in recognising and managing anxious school refusal in collaboration with other agencies within health and social services
- facilitate single agency and inter-agency planning and development of services* for children experiencing anxious school refusal
- assist schools in the management of pupils with similar difficulties
- highlight the problems that may arise when services have different geographical boundaries.

Single agency responses may be insufficient to address the complex and often long-standing problems of children who present with anxious school refusal.

---

* It should be noted that the terms and structures used in this booklet relate to one Local Education Authority (LEA). Different names and structures serving similar purposes may exist in other localities.

The nature and extent of school refusal

A definition of school refusal by Berg, Nichols and Pritchard, which helps distinguish school refusal from truancy, lists the following features:

- Severe difficulty in attending school, often amounting to prolonged absence.
- Severe emotional upset on being faced with the prospect of going to school. This may be shown by excessive fearfulness, anxiety, temper, misery, complaints of feeling ill without obvious cause.
- Staying at home with parental knowledge.
- Absence of significant antisocial disorders, e.g. stealing, destructiveness.

Anxiety may be defined as an exaggerated state of normal fear, an unpleasant state of mind with the expectation, but not the certainty, of something untoward happening. Fish describes it as '... a fear for no adequate reason, which is more than an uneasy preoccupation or worry about something'.

The extent of the problem

Rutter suggests the incidence of school refusal is less than 3%. It is evident that the acute presentation and majority of referrals with school refusal concern secondary school-age pupils and lead mainly to intervention with adolescents. Rarely are significant concerns about anxious school refusal raised by primary schools. However, parents of older children often reveal that reluctance to leave home for school was evident at primary school level, but that such anxieties were not so overwhelming as to result in real concerns about the child's non-attendance. This would suggest that seeds of school refusal are often sown in early childhood but perhaps not always recognised or understood at that point. Therefore, the development of anxious school refusal may not be identified early if frequent short absences from school (i.e. less than three weeks) are authorised as being due to minor ailments, thus masking the real problem.

- The average comprehensive school of approximately 1000 pupils could expect to have 2-3 pupils, at any one time, experiencing anxiety that is adversely affecting their school attendance.
- In addition there may be a greater number of pupils who are anxious about attending school or leaving home, but who are managing to maintain some level of school attendance.

- Problems of separation anxiety are probably more common in the primary school-age group but are more easily contained.

The interventions described in this booklet are applicable to both primary and secondary schools and their pupils. Appropriate intervention may limit the severity and duration of the episode and reduce longer-term problems.

Two fundamental features of school refusal are the presence of anxiety, which can be a great disorganiser of behaviour, and non-attendance at school. The following diagram illustrates the relationship between anxiety and non-attendance.

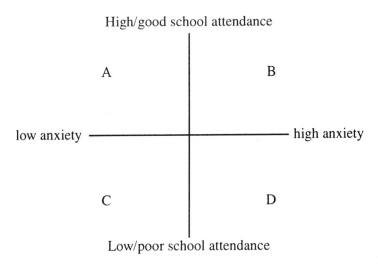

- A - the majority of the school population in that they are not anxious and have good attendance records.
- B - children who are very anxious but do manage to maintain school attendance.
- C - children who may be considered as truants in as much as they have low school attendance but do not show anxiety as the major factor leading to their non-attendance.
- D - children who are highly anxious and feel unable to attend school. These are the children considered to be anxious school refusers.

Classifying children's difficulties is not a simple or straightforward task and there is often blurring or overlapping of the categories.

8

The role of separation anxiety was highlighted by John Bowlby who suggested that, frequently, what a child fears is leaving home, rather than what will happen at school. Bowlby explains how separation anxiety can lead to over-dependence on home. He described four family scenarios from which this problem may arise:

- The child fears something dreadful may happen to a significant attachment figure, usually a parent, grandparent or primary carer, while he/she is at school and so remains at home to prevent it happening.
- A parent may suffer chronic anxiety regarding his or her own attachment figures and retain the child at home to be a companion.
- The child fears something dreadful may happen to himself/herself while at school and so remains at home to prevent it happening.
- A parent fears something dreadful may happen to the child while he/she is at school so keeps him/her at home to prevent it happening.

Generally one pattern dominates, although mixed cases can and do occur.

According to the criteria of the Diagnostic and Statistical Manual of the American Psychiatric Association (DSM IV) **separation anxiety** may be said to be present when, at a developmentally inappropriate age*, a child shows three or more of the following for a period of more than two weeks:

- Unrealistic worry about possible harm befalling major attachment figures or fear that they will leave and not return.
- Unrealistic worry that a calamitous event will separate the child from a major attachment figure, e.g. the child will be lost, kidnapped, killed or the victim of an accident.
- Persistent reluctance or refusal to go to school in order to stay with the major attachment figure at home.
- Persistent reluctance or refusal to go to sleep without being next to a major attachment figure or to go to sleep away from home.
- Persistent avoidance of being alone in the home and emotional upset if unable to follow the major attachment figure around the home.
- Repeated nightmares involving the theme of separation.

---

* Behaviour which may appear 'out of step' with a child's chronological age but would be considered appropriate in a younger child.

- Complaints of physical symptoms on school days.
- Signs of excessive distress upon separation, or when anticipating separation, from major attachment figures, e.g. temper tantrums, crying or pleading with parents not to leave.
- Social withdrawal, apathy, sadness or difficulty concentrating on work or play when not with the major attachment figure.

The picture at home is usually one of distress and unhappiness for all concerned. Parents are frequently despairing, they may feel guilty or blame themselves for their child's anxiety and reluctance to attend school. There can be considerable family conflict. When faced with the prospect of leaving home for school the child may display many apparently irrational behaviours, such as panicking, shaking, crying, or having temper tantrums and resisting all efforts to encourage them to attend school. To others the child may present with feelings of social inferiority, low self-esteem or depression. The child may be experiencing or say he/she is experiencing physical ailments, e.g. headaches, stomach upsets or a range of minor ailments. This can be one reason why early identification of the problem is not straightforward. Parents may authorise such absences, so it may be some time before the real problem is identified.

Lack of understanding of anxious school refusal in families, in schools and other professionals can lead to defensiveness and blaming. Parents may point the finger at schools as the single or major cause of their child's distress and attendance problem and professionals may be too quick to recognise factors outside the school environment. This may lead to the parents feeling blamed. This may, in turn, lead to unnecessary delay in seeking appropriate help and support.

There are various contributory factors, which may increase a child's vulnerability to, or trigger, school refusal. These may include:

- school transfer
- bullying or fear of being bullied
- illness within the family
- traumatic events within the family
- bereavement
- peer group difficulties
- under-recognised learning difficulties
- long-term illness resulting in prolonged absence from school.

Any one, or a combination of these, may make the difference between manageable anxiety and reluctance to attend school and unmanageable anxiety and overt school refusal.

King acknowledges the importance of school-related factors in the development and maintenance of the problem. Social skills deficits are felt to be significant in the maintenance of school refusal because such skills are essential to most areas of school life, i.e. to enable a child to socialise with peers and to approach teachers appropriately. Intermittent absence may also compound the problem, with children aware and anxious about the amount of classwork missed and 'what is being said about them' during their absence from school. Increasingly isolated, a child has few opportunities to learn good coping strategies.

In some cases a child may not excessively fear school but simply finds life at home preferable and more rewarding than school. The extra attention a child receives at home acts as a reinforcer and school appears less appealing.

Due to the multiple and interrelated causative factors, understanding the nature of school refusal is not necessarily easy for children, parents or professionals.

Identification and intervention

The central importance of the school's role in the prevention, early identification and continuing management of school refusal has been increasingly recognised.

Preventative action by the school should be aimed at encouraging and maintaining the attendance of *all* pupils. Such practices emerge from a school's ethos and the general aim of promoting a secure and caring environment for children and young people. Examples of good practice include:

- Clear policies in place regarding behaviour, discipline and bullying - particularly the latter because an incident of bullying is often the 'final straw', which may trigger anxious school refusal but can be perceived as the sole cause of the problem by parents and child.
- Procedures for ensuring that, wherever possible, new intake pupils are placed in teaching and pastoral groups with a friend. This applies to Year 7 pupils and older pupils transferring into the school.
- School councils where pupils have opportunities to voice concerns or identify specific problems, e.g. problems of lunchtime arrangements, school transport etc.
- Welcoming, encouraging and actively supporting links with parents.

Where more direct intervention is required, to prevent barriers being built which can exacerbate the problem, many schools adopt a staged approach in response to children who appear anxious and reluctant to attend school. Initial concern about a child showing anxiety or reluctance to attend can be expressed by a number of people including:

- the student him/herself, being obviously upset
- a concerned friend reporting problems
- a parent/guardian communicating the problems to school
- a form teacher, pastoral manager, e.g. head of year/house, or Education Welfare Officer noticing a significant level or particular pattern of non-attendance, e.g. frequent absence on Mondays or after school holidays.

Early identification is important but is often delayed because the reasons presented by parents to explain or authorise the non-attendance may only partly explain the problem. The most common reason given is that the child was unwell.

At the school-based stages of the *Code of Practice* (School Support, Stages 1 and 2)* a range of intervention measures can be used by individual primary and secondary schools and some examples of good practice are listed below:

- early contact with parents to discuss the child's reluctance to attend school
- encouraging parents to play an active role, e.g. by inviting them to informal reviews in school to discuss the problem, transporting/escorting their child to school
- ensuring the child is appropriately placed in classes, i.e. both socially and academically, and making class, group or seating adjustments if necessary
- ensuring the child has access to an identified member of staff, who can be approached if anxiety becomes temporarily overwhelming in school, e.g. class teacher for primary pupils and head of year for secondary pupils
- encouraging a friend or identified pupil to keep in touch with the anxious child
- investigating concerns about bullying.

School-based support and intervention needs to be reviewed regularly in school. The school and parents, as partners, should monitor attendance. Good communication between pupil, parents and school is central to providing emotional security, enabling the child to attend school. The Education Welfare Officer can assist the maintenance of home-school links.

Where concerns about a child continue (see flowchart) the pastoral lead within school may request a progress report from the pupil's form teacher and subject teachers. Particular attention should be paid to the levels at which the child is working, progress made and any areas of difficulty, either within the curriculum or with peer relationships. Evaluation of this information along with information from other sources, e.g. medical information, problems as reported by parents/carers, any previous or current external agency involvement, can provide a greater understanding of the situation. Further action could involve:

- accurate assessment of learning difficulties
- sending work home to ensure curriculum continuity

---

* Terminology may change with the new *Code of Practice* expected in 2000.

- ensuring any returned work can be seen to be valued, e.g. prompt marking and making comments
- liaison with the Education Welfare Service and other professionals for further information and advice
- home visits or telephone calls by the class teacher, for primary pupils, or a pastoral teacher for secondary pupils, helps to maintain home-school links
- allowing access to a 'safe' place in school where a child could retreat temporarily and work, if overwhelmed by anxiety
- referral to the 'worry clinic' or 'drop in' session that may be organised by the school nurse.

In cases of anxious school refusal, where early intervention at a school level has not led to progress towards re-establishing attendance, it is appropriate to seek multi-agency advice and support. Experience would indicate that early collaborative action can prevent repetition of effort and promote more effective use of limited resources.

Multi-agency involvement
The decision to seek multi-agency involvement may lead to:

- a multi-agency assessment of the problem
- promotion of a common understanding of the areas of difficulty
- formulation of an action plan with realistic targets and timescales, detailing which agencies should become involved and in what capacity (a process essentially the same as drawing up an Individual Education Plan)
- planning and target setting with the child to assist him/her to feel more in control
- persisting with agreed targets despite any setbacks, rather than continually seeking new or alternative 'solutions'
- supporting flexible approaches to timetabling, which may include temporarily allowing some part-time attendance
- alerting all to the need for vigilance following natural breaks, e.g. holidays or genuine illness as anxieties often resurface at such times
- ensuring all staff are informed about the child's difficulties
- circulating a progress report to raise the child's profile within school
- in-service training for school staff about the nature and management of anxious school refusal

- seeking advice and/or support from the LEA's Learning Support Service or Educational Psychology Service, where appropriate. A range of provision may exist within individual LEAs for supporting anxious/school phobic pupils and will be set out in the LEA's Behaviour Support Plan
- a range of therapeutic intervention and support for the child and family from the Child and Adolescent Mental Health Service
- holding regular informal and formal reviews of progress.

Expectations of an 'instant cure' are unhelpful. Anxious pupils need acknowledgement and encouragement for *any* progress made.

The pattern of attendance following initial intervention will need to be monitored. If a significant or increasing number or pattern of absences continues the decision will be made whether or not there has been acceptable progress towards re-establishing the child's attendance. If significant progress has not been made the school should decide whether to move the child through the School-Based Support stages or directly to a Support Plus stage of the Code of Practice. The decision to move to the next stage depends on:

- the change in the level or pattern of absence
- the child's previous attendance record
- the family's perception of the problem
- the level of the child's anxiety
- the effect on the child's learning and out-of-school life.

It is difficult to assign precise timescales because each case is different.

Acute school refusal - a model of response with reference to the Stage Procedures

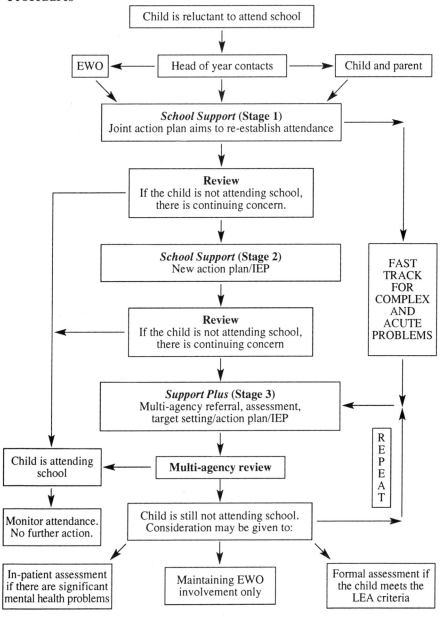

Child is reluctant to attend school

Head of year contacts → EWO

Head of year contacts → Child and parent

School Support (Stage 1)
Joint action plan aims to re-establish attendance

Review
If the child is not attending school, there is continuing concern.

School Support (Stage 2)
New action plan/IEP

Review
If the child is not attending school, there is continuing concern

Support Plus (Stage 3)
Multi-agency referral, assessment, target setting/action plan/IEP

Multi-agency review

Child is attending school

Monitor attendance. No further action.

Child is still not attending school. Consideration may be given to:

FAST TRACK FOR COMPLEX AND ACUTE PROBLEMS

REPEAT

In-patient assessment if there are significant mental health problems

Maintaining EWO involvement only

Formal assessment if the child meets the LEA criteria

Agency boundaries and the roles
of various professionals

The problem of reluctance to attend school, when associated with high levels of anxiety, may rapidly become a multi-agency problem. In order to deal effectively and efficiently with these problems, a clear and co-ordinated multi-agency response is helpful. Working relationships between members of the relevant agencies are important. These are best developed when:

- agencies serve the same geographical area
- staff are clear about their own role
- staff are clear about the roles, responsibilities and limitations of other agencies
- staff value the possibility of an effective multi-agency network
- staff are supported by their own agency in investing in the network.

Each agency has its own catchment territory. These territories will be of differing sizes, with extremes exemplified by:

- primary schools serving a 'village population'
- Child and Adolescent Mental Health Services serving one or more Local Government Districts.

Lack of shared geographical boundaries between Health, Education and Social Services Teams leads to a situation of great complexity, adding considerably to the difficulties faced by professionals in their attempts to help children and families with complex problems. It may mean that networks will need to be established on a case-by-case basis and cannot be underpinned by familiarity and trust in relationships, clear understanding of roles, responsibilities and limitations and a shared understanding of school refusal. With regard to anxious school refusal the relevant agencies include:

Education
- Schools: primary, secondary and special
- Educational Welfare Officers or Education Social Workers
- Educational Psychologists
- Local Education Authority Support Services which may include a Home Teaching Service as part of the Education Otherwise Than At School Service or Learning Support Service.

Health

- School doctors
- School nurses
- GPs
- Child and Adolescent Mental Health Service.

Social Services

- Child Care Team.

The roles of various professionals

The school, along with parents, has a primary role to play with regard to children who are reluctant to attend school. In many cases the school's pastoral care programme and consultation with parents is sufficient to re-establish the regular school attendance of anxious pupils who are reluctant to attend school. However, certain complex cases may require consultation, advice and direct intervention from external agencies.

It is helpful to have a clear understanding of the roles and limitations of the various agencies within a Local Authority that may be involved with children who are anxious and reluctant to attend school. There may be some degree of overlap of roles and responsibilities.

The Education Welfare Officer/Education Social Worker is able to support schools in identifying cases of non-attendance which require further action and will:

- assess circumstances which may have led to the breakdown of school attendance
- identify causes and significant factors which can assist in resolving the problem
- plan action with the child, family and the school, involving specialist agencies, if necessary, aimed at re-establishing attendance
- support the child and family to plan, implement and review strategies that can re-establish school attendance
- maintain records of work
- initiate Court action, in appropriate cases, on behalf of the LEA should the problem remain unresolved.

The Educational Psychologist is able to respond to referrals about anxious pupils and may:

- liaise with schools
- meet with children and families for assessment
- refer to other agencies, if necessary, e.g. Education Welfare Service, LEA's Support Service, or Child and Adolescent Mental Health Service
- initiate formal assessment under the *1996 Education Act*, if necessary
- facilitate communications between other involved agencies
- offer advice and/or support during reintegration into school.

The School Medical Services are able to respond promptly to referrals about anxious pupils who are reluctant to attend. The school doctor may:

- meet with the family and examine the child
- liaise with other medical agencies, e.g. GPs or paediatricians, to obtain appropriate treatment for the child or to exclude physical illness as the main cause of non-attendance
- offer the family advice and support
- communicate with other professionals involved
- refer to another agency, e.g. Child and Adolescent Mental Health Service or the LEA's Support Service if necessary.

The School Nurse is a regular visitor to school and may offer informal 'drop in' sessions on a regular basis, giving pupils direct access to discuss a problem or worry. Pupils may also be referred to the school nurse by teaching or medical staff, by the Education Welfare Officer/Education Social Worker or by the parents of the pupils themselves.

For anxious students attending school, the School Nurse can offer support and advice as well as information. The school nurse can negotiate or liaise on the pupil's behalf, aiming to minimise anxiety and assist the child to develop coping strategies.

Other agencies may be contacted or referrals made with the knowledge and/or consent of the pupil. Home visits can be carried out if appropriate.

Social Services may have a role to play when children who are reluctant to attend school are also considered to be children in need. When referrals are made to Social Services they are initially dealt with by the Information and Assessment Team who may be able to offer a limited assessment and advice. Where the main problem is non-attendance at school the referral is redirected to the Education Welfare Service. Where there are other complex problems, usually associated with behaviour and/or relationships, the referral will be passed to a member of the Child Care Team, who will undertake fuller assessment which will include contacting other agencies involved and the offer of advice and support.

Depending on the assessed need, the Department may provide other services in addition to social work advice, e.g. Home Support Worker, referral to the Therapeutic Team or Day Respite. A child would not normally be accommodated for reasons of non-attendance alone.

The Child and Adolescent Mental Health Service will consider referrals about children who are unwilling to attend school. Referrals are accepted from a range of agencies in Health, Education and Social Services. It is helpful if school refusal is given a high priority. Members of the multi-disciplinary team may:

- meet the child and family for an initial assessment
- liaise with other agencies involved, with the family's consent
- provide psychological treatment and support as indicated and in conjunction with other professionals involved.

There is no statutory basis for the involvement of the Child and Adolescent Mental Health Service and families may be reluctant to attend appointments. 'Clinic refusal' may follow 'school refusal'.

The LEA Support Service, e.g. Home and Hospital Support Service, may be able to support a school's attempts to provide education for children who are refusing to attend school due to high levels of school or home-related anxiety. Section 9 of the *1997 Education Act* states that the LEA's Behaviour Support Plan should give details of services and provision for pupils educated otherwise than at school. LEA Behaviour Support Plans should set out the whole range of local support services offered to specific groups of vulnerable pupils, including school refusers and school phobics. Provision may include individual support towards reintegration into school from a Learning Support Service or Home Teaching Service, temporary placement at a Pupil Referral Unit, School Returner's Unit, small group provision specifically for anxious pupils or alternative educational provision.

Support Services may distinguish between cases of truancy and anxious school refusal. There may be different provision for pupils who are disenchanted with school and who *will not*, as opposed to feeling they *cannot*, attend school.

It is beneficial when LEA Support Services have an open referral system allowing schools parents or other agencies to refer, although in reality the majority of referrals are likely to be made by schools. The LEA Support Service may:

- provide advice and training to schools and other agencies about anxious school refusal and strategies which can assist and maintain a pupil's return to school
- provide advice to children and families
- offer pupils a gradual reintegration into school via individual support
- consult and liaise with other agencies
- provide a number of hours per week direct teaching, possibly at an individual tuition centre/school returners unit or at a Pupil Referral Unit or through individual tuition, usually as part of a structured reintegration programme.

Unless formally registered elsewhere the pupil is likely to remain the responsibility of the school, which continues to receive the Age Weighted Pupil Unit (LEA allocated finance per pupil). The school is, therefore, expected to direct planning of the curriculum and supply resources for the child's continuing education. Following a referral, staff within the LEA Support Service may find it useful to initiate a period of consultation and may:

- gather information by liaison with school, child, family and any other professionals involved
- arrange a multi-agency meeting where appropriate
- clarify and agree with the school, child, family and other agencies the type and purpose of the support proposed, emphasising reintegration into school.

Where an individual teacher from the LEA Support Service is appointed to work with the pupil, it is helpful to jointly plan and set targets with school staff, child, family and other professionals. It is important to ensure regular multi-agency reviews are held in school to discuss progress, set future targets and ensure the appropriateness of on-going support.

Year 9, 10 and 11 pupils should be encouraged to maintain links with the Careers Service. Referral may be made, with parents' permission, to the Child and Adolescent Mental Health Service, if necessary.

Identification of gaps in service provision

Local gaps may be identified in multi-agency provision. This may be especially acute in some localities due to a national shortage of some disciplines and uneven development of services. There may also be some local difficulty in availability of information, training or understanding about anxious school refusal. The gaps in one area may differ from another.

The clinical problem of reluctance to attend school exists on a spectrum. At one end of the spectrum the child's anxieties and expressed reluctance may be contained by parents and school, possibly with some support from an Education Social Worker or Educational Welfare Officer, GP or School Nurse.

At the other end of the spectrum clinical problems presented may be complex, severe, chronic and entrenched. The professional network may have expanded to include direct involvement with School Doctors, Educational Psychologists, LEA Support Services, and Child and Adolescent Mental Health Services. To this expanded network may be added input from Social Services Departments, Child Care and Child Protection Teams.

As the problem becomes more severe, so the gaps in provision become more apparent and disadvantageous to the child. This may be particularly noticeable where there is a lack of resources, where agency boundaries are not co-terminous or there is a lack of effective multi-agency partnerships. Shortages of staff in Child and Adolescent Mental Health Services, coupled with high levels of demand for services, means that children may have to wait many months for assessment of a clinical problem that is increasingly compounded by secondary educational handicap through prolonged non-attendance. During this period the central role and active concern of the school may be lost.

It appears that understanding of the problem is patchy. The underlying role of anxiety, including separation anxiety, and the role of the family may not be well understood.

There may be a lack of dedicated Pupil Referral Unit facilities to assist in the management of children whose reluctance to attend school may have an anxiety base.

There may be little strategic multi-agency planning of future provision for this group of children.

Guidelines for future action

Improving understanding and recognition of the nature of anxious school refusal is fundamental to future developments. Schools, as the main referral agency where reluctance to attend is concerned, need to have a clear understanding of the nature of the problem in order to determine which cases may require a rapid multi-agency response. Such awareness-raising may be needed for other front line agencies such as the Educational Welfare Service.

Awareness-raising could be achieved through in-service training, possibly on a multi-agency basis which would need to include the following elements:

- definition of school refusal/reluctance to attend and essential features
- differential diagnosis - how to distinguish truancy from refusal
- an awareness of the complexity of the problem and the interaction of individual, family and environmental factors
- a recognition of the importance of early identification and intervention
- an understanding of the roles of the various agencies that may be involved in cases of reluctance to attend
- the production of written information about anxious school refusal for schools, other agencies, parents, children and young people.

A proactive approach is likely to be more successful than crisis management when the refusal has become entrenched. 'Wait and see' is rarely a wise approach when reluctance to attend is concerned. Schools should not delay in moving to Stage 3 or Support Plus if interventions at earlier stages are met with little or no success.

There should be **clear information** about the extent of available support within a Local Authority, including how advice can be obtained and how a referral can be made. The information should give details about the level of local provision schools and families can expect to receive.

There should be **strategic joint agency planning** for this group of children and young people. This will require direct input from the relevant parties in Education, Health and Social Services. Plans should include the resourcing of appropriate facilities and staff training. Joint agency funding would further this development. Recent changes in legislation with regard to joint agency funding should facilitate these developments.

Local Education Authorities, Health Authorities and Social Services Departments may wish to address problems arising from a lack of shared geographical boundaries for local services as a means of strengthening partnerships and local networking.

LEAs have a duty to ensure these pupils do not lose out on opportunities to continue and complete their education.

The co-ordination of existing services

Whose responsibility?

The problem of anxious school refusal is not solely a school, health or social problem, nor is it amenable to quick or magical solutions. Successful management depends on mobilising an appropriate, timely and co-ordinated multi-agency response that is integrated and coherent.

There needs to be a clear understanding that schools retain the ultimate responsibility for the pupil. Where acute problems arise schools should alert agencies, seek their advice or involvement and co-ordinate subsequent responses. Recognition of the school's central role is crucial if confusion and lack of direction are to be avoided.

Within individual non-school-based agencies there exists substantial experience in the management of anxious school refusal. In many cases progress has been made towards joint agency working, replacing single agency endeavours that may be uncoordinated, and lead to duplication of efforts, confusion and sometimes even conflict.

An effective mechanism for joint agency consultation is required, geared to the need for early intervention in order to reduce the need for prolonged multi-agency involvement. Schools can be assisted with their management of anxious school refusal through access to joint consultation and advice.

A model for specialist joint consultation, facilitation and advice

The authors are a manager of an LEA Home and Hospital Support Service and a Child and Family Psychiatrist. Different combinations would be likely to evolve in other localities. What is required is a wide range of knowledge, skills and experience from different professional backgrounds and systems alongside a commitment to develop effective partnerships.

A consultation service should be readily accessible, with a clear system for referral. It may be helpful to circulate schools and the Education Welfare Service with a pre-arranged timetable of dates available for consultation throughout the academic year.

Once a school has decided it wishes to arrange a joint consultation there will need to be discussion about who should be invited to attend a school-based meeting. The composition will vary from case to case but should always include school-based staff (Pastoral Manager and/or Special Educational Needs Co-ordinator (SENCO)), Educational Welfare Officer, and parents/carers. It may be helpful to include the pupil in the consultation process (they will not always attend). Others should be invited as appropriate and might include School Medical Officer or School Nurse, GP, Educational Psychologist, Child and Adolescent Mental Health Personnel, LEA Support Service Personnel and Social Services Personnel.

The consultation meetings provide an opportunity for presentation and exploration of the case with the following aims:

- to carry out some assessment of the situation
- to achieve a common understanding of the difficulty
- to determine whether the problem is one of reluctance to attend
- to form an action plan with realistic targets and timescales and specify which agencies should become involved and in what capacity (a process essentially the same as drawing up an Individual Education Plan).

Subsequent meetings to monitor progress involve the relevant subgroup of the initial consultation group.

By bringing together in school a range of professionals with different expertise, the consultation can provide an opportunity to clarify complex situations and inform future school-based or multi-agency plans. The consultation process needs to be able to create a forum where there can be containment of insecurity and anxiety and where reasonable outcomes can be discussed and planned. Clear plans with explicit responsibilities are appreciated so that everyone knows what is due to happen next.

The consultation potentially puts parents and teachers on a more equal footing and provides an opportunity to clarify misunderstandings. It is useful to have discussion with a variety of people, as the perceptions of teachers are often different from those of the child or parent. Consultations may be able to 'fill in the gaps' for schools who may previously have been attempting to solve a problem without being aware of its nature or full extent. The consultations can provide a 'one stop shop', speed up the communication process and provide an opportunity to share good practice among schools.

This forum potentially provides access to a range of advice, interventions and services. It is aimed at supporting the development of understanding of anxious school refusal and, where necessary, refocusing existing efforts of schools, families and other agencies. Direct input from Education Welfare Service, Learning Support Service, Child and Adolescent Mental Health Service (CAMHS), other agencies or a combination as appropriate can be accessed as required. The consultation process re-emphasises and supports the school's central role and does not present a quick fix solution.

Conclusion

Children who experience problems with separation anxiety and school refusal may have long-standing and entrenched difficulties. Family problems may be trans-generational and complex. The efforts of schools and other professionals may be easily frustrated. It is the authors' belief that significant future harm to children's emotional, social and cognitive development can best be avoided through a co-ordinated multi-agency response aimed at maximising their successful reintegration, educationally and socially, promoting their emotional development and reducing the likelihood of mental health problems persisting into adult life.

References

Berg, I., Nichols, K. and Pritchard, C. (1969) 'School phobia - its classification and relationship to dependency.' *Journal of Child Psychology and Psychiatry,* 10. Cambridge University Press: Cambridge.

Bowlby, J. (1973) Attachment and Loss: Volume 2 Separation Anxiety and Anger. Penguin: London.

Department for Education (1994) *The Code of Practice on the Identification and Assessment of Special Educational Needs.* HMSO: London.

Diagnostic and Statistical Manual of Mental Disorders 4th Edition (DSM IV) Washington DC American Psychiatric Association (1994).

Hamilton, M. (1981) 'Fish's Clinical Psychopathology.' John Wright & Sons Ltd.: Bristol.

King, N. J., Hamilton, D. I. and Ollendick, T. H. (1994) 'Children's Phobias: A Behavioural Perspective.' John Wiley and Sons Ltd.: Chichester.

Philbrick, D. and Tansey, K. (Eds.) (June 1998) 'School Refusal: Children who are anxious and reluctant to attend school.' A report of the multi-agency working party in the Central Durham area. Durham.

Rutter, M., Tizard, J. and Whitmore, K. (Eds.) (1970) 'The Isle of Wight Study', in Education, Health and Behaviour. Longman: Harlow.